People of the Bible and Their Prayers

People of the Bible
and Their Prayers

Written by Gloria Truitt
Illustrated by Alice Hausner

W9-AMO-362

ARCH® Books

Copyright © 1987 Concordia Publishing House
3558 S. Jefferson Avenue, St. Louis, MO   63118-3968
Manufactured in the United States of America

God Speaks Through Us

Moses Prays for Eloquence—
Exodus 4:10–16

Moses was surprised and scared
    when God said, "You will be
The one to free the Israelites
    from Pharaoh's slavery."
"Oh, Lord, my speech is very slow!
    I can't do what You ask!

I pray, send someone else instead
    of me to do this task."
God said, "Your brother, Aaron, I
    will send along with you,
And I will speak through both your mouths,
    and teach you what to do."

Lord, Strengthen Me!

Samson Prays to Avenge His Enemies—Judges 16:28

Samson was a faithful man
    whose hair was long in length.
He fought the warring Philistines
    with his amazing strength.
But when Delilah cut his hair,
    he lost his super might.
Then he was captured by his foes
    who took away his sight.
He prayed to God to be avenged,
    "O Lord God, strengthen me!"
And with that prayer God granted him
    one last, great victory!

The Childless Wife

Hannah's Prayer for a Son—
1 Samuel 1:10–11

Hannah was a childless wife,
    and so she felt quite sad.
If only she could have a son,
    her heart would then be glad!

She went into the temple and
    prayed silently one day,
"Lord, if You bless me with a son,
    from You he'll never stray!"
Not only did God grant her wish,
    but children, five in all!
Indeed, her firstborn, Samuel,
    through life obeyed God's call!

Make Me Wise!

Solomon's Prayer for Wisdom—
1 Kings 3:6–9

King Solomon was ruling when
    his dad, King David, died.
"I'm far too young, not smart enough
    to be a king," he cried.
"Oh, Lord," he prayed, "please make me wise!
    Oh, tell me what to do!"

Because he prayed not for himself,
    God gave him riches, too,
And told him he would be most wise,
    like none who'd gone before.
Because this king loved God so much,
    God gave him *so* much more!

God Answers Hezekiah

Hezekiah's Prayer for Renewed Health— 2 Kings 20:1–6

Hezekiah was a king,
    a king about to die.
So sick was he, all he could do
    was pray to God and cry.
But then his friend, Isaiah, came
    to visit him one day.

God told this friend to tell the king,
"I hear the words you pray.
You've always walked in faithfulness,
and now I see your tears,
So I will make you well again,
and grant you fifteen years!"

Saved from the Sea

Jonah's Prayer of Thanksgiving— Jonah 2

Jonah was a drowning man,
    and terribly afraid,
But God had work for him to do,
    so He came to his aid.

God sent a monstrous, giant fish
    to swallow up this man,
And carry him to safety where
    he'd spit him out on land.
While Jonah was inside this fish
    he prayed a thank-You prayer;
For truly God had saved him through
    His great and loving care.

Mary's Prayer of Praise

The Magnificat—Luke 1:46–55

Before the birth of Jesus Christ,
  Elizabeth told Mary,
"You are the mother of my Lord . . .
  this child that you now carry!

You truly are the favored one!
   To think you are my guest!"
And with that greeting Mary prayed,
   "Oh, Father, I am blest!
For You have done great things to me."
   Then Mary did exclaim,
"How I rejoice in God, my Lord,
   and praise His holy name!"

Salvation I Have Seen

Simeon's Prayer of Contentment—
Luke 2:29–32

A righteous man called Simeon
    was very, very old.
"You will not die till you see Christ,"
    by God this man was told.
One day while he was in God's house,
    the Christ Child was brought in.
He knew at once this holy Child
    would free the world from sin.
"Holy God, You kept Your word,"
    he thanked the Lord on high:
"Because salvation I have seen,
    in peace I now can die."

The Sinner's Prayer

The Pharisee and the Tax Collector—
Luke 18:9–14

Once there was a tax collector
    and a Pharisee.
The first man recognized his sin.
    The second? No, not he!
"I'm perfect!" prayed the Pharisee,
    "and not like others who
Are stingy folks with sinful ways,
    who cheat their neighbors, too."

The tax collector prayed to God
    (his head was humbly bowed),
"Be merciful to me," he prayed—
    he wasn't false or proud.
Whom did the Lord forgive that day?
    No, not the Pharisee!
The Lord forgave that humble man
    who sinned like you and me!

Make Them One As We Are One

Jesus Prays for Us—John 17

Our Lord and Savior, Jesus Christ,
    prayed each and every day,
While teaching those who followed Him
    to walk the righteous way.
In chapter seventeen of John,
    He prayed for everyone—
Everyone who'd known Him as
    God's only chosen Son.
Because He knew He'd leave this earth,
    this was a special prayer:
"Make them one as We are one,
    and keep them in Your care."

God's Great Love

Paul's Prayer for the Ephesians—Ephesians 3:14–21

The greatest of Christ's messengers
    was one apostle, Paul.
Although he was imprisoned, Paul
    stayed true to Jesus' call.

He wrote a letter while in jail,
    repeating what he'd prayed.
"We all belong to Christ," he said.
    "Be strong and not afraid!
There is no end to God's great love,
    no height, no depth, nor length;
And through His Spirit He'll give you
    a mighty inner strength!"

DEAR PARENTS:

Prayer is not an option for the Christian. God wants us to call on Him in every need: "Call upon Me in the day of trouble. I will deliver thee, and thou shalt glorify Me" (Psalm 50:15).

But a time of crisis is not the only time to pray. We can, and should, as Paul tells the Thessalonians, "pray without ceasing. In everything give thanks; for this is the will of God in Christ Jesus concerning you."

Prayer is the heartbeat of the sanctified life. It is our constant companion, whether openly expressed or inwardly felt. "You cannot find a Christian without prayer, just as you cannot find a living man without a pulse" was the way Luther described prayer in the Christian life.

Ask the Holy Spirit to help you model for your child a faithful life of prayer. Ask Him to help you share with your child the joy and comfort and importance of this most intimate and direct contact with our heavenly Father. The apostle Paul expressed it well: "Do not be anxious about anything, but in everything, by prayer and petition, with thanksgiving, present your requests to God" (Philippians 4:6 NIV).

THE EDITOR